LIBRARY
STREET
2227

D1541406

SUPERSTARS

of
PRO
FOOTBALL

TONY ROMO

Chuck Bednar

Mason Crest Publishers

Produced by OTTN Publishing in association with
21st Century Publishing and Communications, Inc.

Copyright © 2009 by Mason Crest Publishers. All rights reserved. No part of this
publication may be reproduced or transmitted in any form or by any means,
electronic or mechanical, including photocopying, recording, taping, or any
information storage and retrieval system, without permission from the publisher.

MASON CREST PUBLISHERS INC.
370 Reed Road
Broomall, Pennsylvania 19008
(866) MCP-BOOK (toll free)
www.masoncrest.com

Printed in the United States of America.

First Printing

9 8 7 6 5 4 3 2 1

Library of Congress Cataloging-in-Publication Data

Bednar, Chuck, 1976–
  Tony Romo / Chuck Bednar.
    p. cm. — (Superstars of pro football)
  Includes bibliographical references.
ISBN 978-1-4222-0540-2 (hardcover) — ISBN 978-1-4222-0835-9 (pbk.)
  1. Romo, Tony, 1980–   2. Football players—United States—Biography.
3. Quarterbacks (Football)—United States—Biography. I. Title.
GV939.R646B43 2008
796.332092—dc22
[B]   1025110   2008025393

Publisher's note:
All quotations in this book come from original sources, and contain the spelling
and grammatical inconsistencies of the original text.

◀◀ **CROSS-CURRENTS** ▶▶

In the ebb and flow of the currents of life we are each influenced
by many people, places, and events that we directly experience or
have learned about. Throughout the chapters of this book you will
come across **CROSS-CURRENTS** reference bubbles. These bubbles
direct you to a **CROSS-CURRENTS** section in the back of the
book that contains fascinating and informative sidebars
and related pictures. Go on. ▶▶

◀◀CONTENTS▶▶

ELY PUBLIC LIBRARY
1595 DOWS STREET
ELY, IA 52227

THANKSGIVING DAY MVP

CROSS-CURRENTS

For a short history of how the NFL's tradition of Thanksgiving Day football began, and how the Dallas Cowboys have fared on Thanksgiving, see page 47. ▶▶

Thanksgiving Day is traditionally a time for food, family, faith, and football. It's a time for people to take stock of their lives, count their blessings, and express their gratitude for the good things they enjoy. On Thanksgiving Day of 2006, Tony Romo of the Dallas Cowboys certainly had reasons to be thankful.

Just a few weeks earlier, Tony had been named his team's starting quarterback. He had spent three and a half years on the bench—working, watching, learning, and waiting for his chance to

Texas Stadium at Irving is abuzz with excitement before the start of the Dallas Cowboys' Thanksgiving Day game against the Tampa Bay Buccaneers, November 23, 2006. That day, Tony Romo—making only his fifth regular-season start as a professional—would emerge as one of the NFL's brightest young quarterbacks.

take the reins of the Cowboys' offense. At many points it seemed he would never get that chance. But his perseverance had finally paid off.

Trial by Fire

Going into the November 23 game between Dallas and the Tampa Bay Buccaneers, Tony had been the Cowboy starting QB for little over a month. He had played fairly well during that five-game stretch. But this would be an entirely different situation. This was Thanksgiving, and it was a tradition for the Cowboys to play—and play well—on this day. Plus, the game was nationally televised. So in addition to the more than 63,000 fans in attendance at Texas Stadium in Irving,

His eyes focused on a receiver downfield, Tony is ready to deliver a pass. In the 2006 Thanksgiving Day game, he completed 22 of 29 pass attempts for 306 yards, earning a nearly perfect passer rating of 148.9. He also threw for five touchdowns, tying a Dallas Cowboys single-game record.

millions more would be watching the game at home as they enjoyed their turkey, stuffing, and cranberry sauce. The pressure was on.

Early in the game, it appeared that the pressure might prove too much for the young Cowboy quarterback to handle. Tampa Bay scored a **touchdown** on the first possession of the game. With his team trailing 7-0, Tony led the Dallas offense onto the field. After connecting with tight end Jason Witten and wide receiver Terrell Owens for short passes, Tony proceeded to miss an open Terry Glenn for what could have been a touchdown. On the next play, he held the ball too long and was sacked. The Cowboys were forced to punt.

After Dallas got the ball back, Owens beat his defender on a deep route. But Tony underthrew the pass. Another golden opportunity had been missed. Tony seemed headed for a rough game.

On the very next play, however, he found Owens for an 18-yard gain. Tony proceeded to drive Dallas down to the Tampa Bay 30-yard line. Then he hit Glenn deep over the middle for a touchdown.

After the Dallas defense forced a turnover, Tony led the Cowboys on another scoring drive. He connected on four of six pass **attempts**, including a two-yard touchdown toss to Glenn. Then, with time running out in the first half, Tony hit Marion Barber from one yard out. Tony had recorded the first three-touchdown game of his career—and there was still an entire half left to play. More important, thanks to the young quarterback's fine play, the Cowboys took a 21-10 lead into the locker room at halftime.

A Reason to Be Thankful

In the second half, Tony threw two more touchdown passes—one to Barber and one to Owens. His five-touchdown performance paced Dallas to a 38-10 win over the Buccaneers. It also tied a Dallas Cowboys record for most touchdown passes in a single game. By any measure, this would have been a great day. But Tony had done more than throw a bunch of touchdowns. He completed 22 of his 29 pass attempts (and at one point connected on 13 passes in a row), racked up 306 total passing yards, and earned an almost perfect **passer rating** of 148.9 in the process.

Football insiders took notice. Among them was Tony's teammate Terrell Owens. A 10-year veteran of the National Football League

Tony grins as he receives the "Galloping Gobbler Award" from Fox Sports as the Thanksgiving Day MVP. Although the trophy is bestowed in a tongue-in-cheek manner, Tony's performance caught the attention of serious football people. "The sky is the limit for this guy," veteran wide receiver Terrell Owens raved after the game.

(NFL), Owens knew a thing or two about talented quarterbacks. As he told NFL.com after the game:

> **"The sky is the limit for the guy. He's poised back there in the pocket. He makes things happen on the run. He makes great decisions and he's managing the game. He's exceeding expectations right now."**

Romo's coach, the notoriously gruff Bill Parcells, was a little more conservative with his praise. When asked about his quarterback's performance on Thanksgiving, Parcells told Nick Eatman of Dallas-Cowboys.com:

> **"[Romo's] execution is good. . . . I'm impressed [by] the fact that he didn't turn the ball over and he's managing the game well. And that's what he's supposed to do. I think he's a football guy, and he's interest[ed] in playing well. But we've got a ways to go here. So put the anointing oil away."**

Perhaps it *was* a little early to proclaim Tony Romo the next great Dallas Cowboys quarterback. After all, it was only his sixth start in the NFL. He had made plenty of mistakes going into that November 23 game, and he would make many more in the future. However, Tony's record-setting Thanksgiving performance helped convince many Cowboys fans that the franchise had finally found a quarterback the team could count on for many years to come. Dallas had lacked stability at the position since the retirement of Hall of Famer Troy Aikman in 2001. During his 12-year career, Aikman had led "America's Team"—as the Cowboys had been dubbed—to Super Bowl victories in 1993, 1994, and 1996. Since then, Dallas had failed to get back to the NFL's championship game.

Tony Romo's MVP-type performance against the Buccaneers gave the Cowboys' faithful reason to hope that the dry spell might come to an end soon. For Dallas fans, that truly was something to be thankful for.

SUCCESS ON THE SMALL STAGE

Antonio Ramiro Romo was born on April 21, 1980, in San Diego, California. He was the youngest child of Ramiro and Joan Romo, joining sisters Danielle and Jossalyn. When Tony was two, the family relocated to Burlington, Wisconsin. Burlington was a small town of under 10,000 residents that was known for its chocolate factory.

Tony discovered a love for sports at an early age. Despite the fact that he lived less than 150 miles from the city of Green Bay, Tony didn't grow up as a fan of the Packers. Nor was Brett Favre, the great Packers quarterback, his idol. As the quarterback for the Burlington high school football team, Tony wore

From a young age, Tony Romo loved to compete, and he excelled in a number of sports. As a student at Burlington High School in Burlington, Wisconsin, Tony was a standout in basketball as well as football. Hoping to hone his skills in both sports, he studied tapes of all-time greats.

the number 16 in honor of former San Francisco 49ers quarterback Joe Montana.

Flying Under the Radar

As a youngster, Tony played all kinds of sports. Eventually he settled on football, basketball, and golf as his favorites. Tony had a passion for athletic competition. In high school, when he was a standout football and basketball star for the Burlington Demons, he frequently watched tape of great players in both sports. He also read books about the sports' legendary athletes. As former Burlington football coach Steve Gerber later told the *Milwaukee Journal Sentinel*:

> **"He studied so much. . . . He was gifted, but he made a lot of his gifts. He would visualize a lot of things and he would come in and suggest things we could do differently out of a certain formation."**

Tony garnered all-county honors on the **gridiron** (and received an all-state honorable mention in basketball). Yet he was unable to lead Burlington to a winning record in football during his senior season. Partly because of this, he was not highly recruited by colleges. He barely got a look from the nearby University of Wisconsin—or from any other Division I-A college football program, for that matter. Tony later told Jason Wilde of *JG-TC Online* that he understood why he was overlooked:

> **"I would never have recruited me. I mean, I was an average quarterback. I did some things, I ran around and made some plays, but I didn't throw the football very well, [was] a little undersized, all those things. There was nothing that said, 'Hey, go get this guy.'"**

For a while, it appeared that Tony might enroll at Wisconsin-Whitewater, a small Division III school. But then Roy Wittke, the offensive coordinator for the Division I-AA Eastern Illinois Panthers, got a look at Tony on film. Wittke decided to bring him to Eastern Illinois. Tony enrolled at Eastern Illinois University in the fall of 1998.

Small-School Superstar

During his first year at Eastern Illinois, Tony was a **redshirt**. The following season, he played in only three games for the Panthers. Among the coaching staff, there was some doubt about Tony's ability to be successful at the quarterback position. In fact, Panthers head coach Bob Spoo had considered moving Tony to tight end, but Wittke talked him out of this. Though Tony was a bit undersized and didn't have great speed, he worked hard, studied hard, and improved as a football player. That effort, Wittke later told the *Dallas Morning News*, was what eventually earned Tony his chance to start.

Tony wasted little time cashing in on his opportunity. In 2000, as a third-year sophomore, he threw for more than 2,500 yards and 27 touchdowns, earning All–Ohio Valley Conference honors and

CROSS-CURRENTS

Eastern Illinois University, located in Charleston, has produced a number of famous figures in addition to Tony Romo. For details, go to page 49. ▶▶

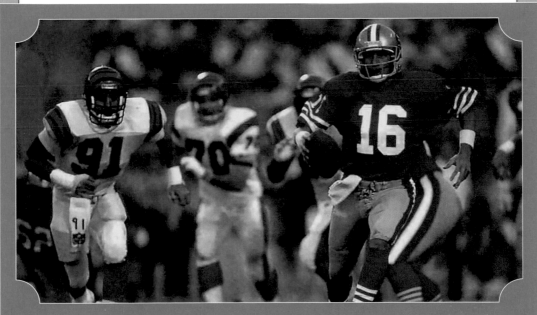

San Francisco 49ers legend Joe Montana scrambles away from defenders. Montana, rather than Green Bay Packers great Brett Favre, was Tony Romo's childhood idol—even though Tony grew up in Wisconsin, less than 150 miles from Green Bay's hallowed Lambeau Field. As a high school quarterback, Tony wore number 16 in honor of Montana.

Sean Payton, seen here as head coach of the New Orleans Saints, was a Dallas Cowboys assistant in 2003, when Tony Romo finished his college career. Payton, who had also been a quarterback at Eastern Illinois University, tried unsuccessfully to convince Cowboys head coach Bill Parcells and team owner Jerry Jones to draft Tony.

bringing home the OVC Player of the Year Award. Tony would repeat both feats as a junior, while also leading Division I-AA quarterbacks in passing efficiency. However, it was as a senior that Tony really shone. He threw for 2,950 yards and 33 touchdowns in 2002, leading Eastern Illinois into the playoffs and winning the Walter Payton Award as the best offensive player in all of Division I-AA. In Spoo's view, Romo was a fitting recipient of the award:

> **"Walter Payton exemplified what dedication and commitment can accomplish. Tony is a classic example of what can be achieved by following Payton's qualities. Tony earned the respect of his teammates by his work ethic. No matter how much individual success he achieved, he still was one of the hardest working players right up to his final collegiate game."**

Finding His Way to the NFL

For all his success at Eastern Illinois, Tony was pretty much off the radar entering the 2003 National Football League **draft**. However, he had caught the attention of Sean Payton, a former quarterback at Eastern Illinois who had once held the school record for most career touchdown passes, with 75. Tony had broken the mark in his senior year, finishing his career with 84 touchdown passes. Payton was now an assistant coach at Dallas.

Payton and Cowboys scout Jim Hess encouraged new Dallas head coach Bill Parcells and Cowboys owner Jerry Jones to draft Tony Romo. But their pleas fell on deaf ears. Tony went undrafted. On May 1, 2003, however, he signed with Dallas as a **free agent**.

It was an inauspicious start to his professional career, yet for Tony the scenario was familiar. He had been overlooked by the major college football programs. Still, he had managed to have a successful collegiate career on the Division I-AA level. Now, thanks to his hard work at Eastern Illinois, he had overcome the criticisms and found his way to the NFL, where he would face the same challenges. Would Tony be able to overcome obstacles again? Only time would tell.

CROSS-CURRENTS

Tony Romo went undrafted in 2003. But that year's class of college quarterbacks included some highly touted prospects. For a full rundown, see page 50. ▶▶

LIFE ON THE NFL SIDELINES

In the fall of 2003, there was a quarterback controversy in Dallas. New head coach Bill Parcells spent the off-season mini-camps evaluating former Georgia Bulldogs quarterback and second-round draft choice Quincy Carter and second-year passer Chad Hutchinson, a product of Stanford University. Tony Romo was just trying to make the team. But even that appeared to be an uphill battle.

Despite all the success Tony had enjoyed in college, Parcells almost immediately detected problems with his throwing motion. Tony delivered the ball with a three-quarters sidearm

As Tony entered his first training camp in the fall of 2003, there seemed little chance that he would find a roster spot with the Dallas Cowboys. Dallas already had two good quarterback prospects, Quincy Carter and Chad Hutchinson, and Tony's throwing mechanics left much to be desired.

motion, rather than a fully overhand motion. This meant that he was releasing the ball at a lower point. In college that hadn't been a major problem for Tony. But Parcells knew that in the NFL—where defensive linemen are on average taller and quicker than their collegiate counterparts—a lot of Tony Romo's pass attempts would be batted down. Tony and Cowboys assistant coach David Lee set to work correcting this flaw. It would be a long, arduous process. The duo worked together before practice each day, and slowly but surely Tony's throwing mechanics began to improve. That, plus the way he impressed coaches with his trademark work ethic, led the Dallas Cowboys to

CROSS-CURRENTS

Tony's first NFL head coach, Bill Parcells, was known for getting the most from his players. A profile of "the Big Tuna" can be found on page 52. ▶▶

keep Tony Romo on the roster as their third quarterback, behind Carter and Hutchinson.

Welcome to the NFL

Tony's first NFL action came in a preseason game against the Arizona Cardinals on August 9, 2003. On his first play, he hit a fellow **rookie**, tight end Jason Witten, for a 12-yard gain. Tony completed his first three pass attempts, then tossed three consecutive incomplete passes. He also threw an interception, leading to a score that cost Dallas its first preseason shutout in nearly a decade. Tony finished the game with lackluster statistics: he completed four of eight passes for 51 yards, had no touchdowns, and threw one interception. He was also sacked once.

In his second outing, Tony threw a 60-yard scoring pass. He finished the preseason having completed 9 of 17 passes for 134 yards and one touchdown. When DallasCowboys.com writer Cliff Cook asked the rookie quarterback about the differences between college football and the NFL, Tony responded:

> **"It's definitely a different atmosphere. We've got as many people [at training camp practices] as we did at my home games. It's easier to practice because you have energy all the time and there's always intensity."**

Tony didn't see any action during the 2003 regular season. He spent the entire year as the third quarterback on the Dallas roster. Carter had won the starting job and was backed up by Hutchinson. Thanks largely to the efforts of the top-ranked defense in the NFL, Dallas recorded a 10-6 record and gained a playoff berth in Parcells's first year as the Cowboys' head coach. In the first round of the play-offs, however, Dallas lost to the Carolina Panthers.

Though Tony had been a spectator throughout the 2003 season, the solid progress he had made working with Lee during practice sessions impressed his coaches. As Sean Payton told Engel:

> **"He kind of lives, breathes football. He's got a quick release. You saw that early on when he first got there. But there were some things he had to work on, some of**

Tony rolls out and looks downfield for an open receiver. As the Cowboys' third quarterback, Tony saw no game action in 2003 after the preseason. In his first preseason appearance—which came in a game against the Arizona Cardinals—Tony's performance was spotty. He completed his first three passes but then threw three straight incomplete passes. He was also intercepted once.

Quincy Carter was the Dallas Cowboys' number-one quarterback in 2003. But only a week into training camp the following year, Carter was unexpectedly cut by head coach Bill Parcells. Still, in his effort to make the 2004 roster, Tony Romo faced another uphill battle, as Parcells had brought in veteran QB Vinnie Testaverde and much-hyped newcomer Drew Henson.

his decisions. He tended to force some balls. . . . [But] he's come a long way."

Chaos at Quarterback

Tony had indeed come a long way in a short time. Nonetheless, during the off-season, his future in the NFL looked bleak. Although the Cowboys cut Chad Hutchinson, they signed veteran NFL quarterback Vinnie Testaverde and traded a third-round draft pick for the rights to former Michigan Wolverines quarterback Drew Henson.

Testaverde was a Parcells favorite—a battle-tested veteran who had played for Parcells with the New York Jets in 1998 and 1999. Henson, a much-hyped prospect at the University of Michigan, had been drafted by the Houston Texans in 2003 but had instead decided to pursue a major-league baseball career. When that didn't work out, Henson opted to try his hand at pro football, and Houston shipped him off to Dallas.

Thus, going into training camp, three quarterbacks were ahead of Tony Romo on the Cowboys' depth chart: 2003 starter Quincy Carter, who had led the team to a 10-victory season and a playoff berth; Testaverde, a proven leader; and Henson, who appeared to have a great deal of potential. That basically left Tony as the odd man out. As Engel observed in his book:

> **There was no way the Cowboys would keep four quarterbacks. And there was no way Romo would clear waivers and be added to the team's practice squad. As it stood, Romo looked to be the most easily squeezed and therefore released by the Cowboys at the end of training camp. The only thing that might save him was if one of the three in front of him suffered an injury.**
>
> **What happened next was far more unpredictable than [if] a sprained ankle or sore shoulder happened.**

What happened next was that the team released Quincy Carter just a week into the 2004 training camp. The reason remains a source of debate. Some reports say that Carter was let go because he failed a drug test. Others suggest that he reacted poorly to the signing of Testaverde, causing locker-room turmoil. Still others claim that he was playing badly and that Parcells wanted to make a statement that no one on the team was 100 percent safe. Whatever the reason, Tony Romo had been granted a reprieve. His days with the Dallas Cowboys weren't over after all. Once again, he would enter the preseason as the number-three quarterback on the roster.

Sophomore Season

The 2004 preseason was a mixed bag for Tony. In his first action, against the Houston Texans on August 8, he was simply awful. Tony threw a pair of interceptions. He was also sacked twice, with one of those sacks coming in his own **end zone** for a Houston safety. The following week, against the Oakland Raiders, Tony scored the game-winning touchdown on a short run. In all, he completed 24 of 39 preseason pass attempts for 250 yards and one touchdown. He was also picked off twice. Still, Tony opened the 2004 regular season as the backup quarterback—although this had less to do with his performance than with the inexperience of Henson. Many observers expected that, as Henson learned the Cowboys' offensive scheme, he would be promoted to backup—and from that role, that he would be groomed as Testaverde's eventual successor.

After the sixth game, Tony indeed lost the backup job to Henson, returning to his familiar role as the third quarterback on the depth chart. Tony did see some regular-season action, but not at the quarterback position: he took over for punter Mat McBriar as the Cowboys' **holder** on **field goal** and **extra point** attempts. It wasn't exactly the stuff of dreams, but at least Tony was getting into games.

Meanwhile, quarterback play remained a weak link in the Dallas offense. Testaverde opened the season as the starter but struggled. The Cowboys' record stood at 3-7, and the team had lost three consecutive games, when Parcells decided to start Henson at quarterback on Thanksgiving Day. But in that game, against the Chicago Bears, Henson played so poorly that Parcells pulled him before the end of the third quarter. Testaverde came off the bench to rally the Cowboys to a pair of fourth-quarter touchdowns and a win. By the final game of the year, Henson had once again surrendered his backup status to Tony Romo. In what could only be described as an eminently forgettable season, the Cowboys finished with a 6-10 record, falling to third place in the NFC East division and failing to return to the playoffs.

Tony spent most of his first three pro seasons riding the bench. Such a situation could have been very frustrating, but Tony always tried to maintain a positive outlook. He never complained, and he worked hard in practice, hoping to be ready if he ever got a chance to take the reins of the Cowboys' offense.

Although he won the role of backup quarterback in 2005, Tony failed to throw a single pass during the entire regular season. In fact, as his third season in a Dallas Cowboys uniform came to an end, Tony had yet to throw a pass in a game that counted. He began to wonder whether he would ever get a shot.

And the Waiting Continues

With such fierce competitors as Jerry Jones and Bill Parcells running the show in Dallas, there was little doubt that the Cowboys would make changes after the disheartening 2004 campaign. But for Tony, the more things changed, the more they stayed the same. Vinnie Testaverde was let go during the off-season. But another Parcells favorite, former New England Patriots quarterback Drew Bledsoe, was brought in to serve as the team's new starter. Drew Henson and Tony Romo battled during training camp to win the role of Bledsoe's backup.

Tony continued to work with Coach Lee, and by this point his mechanics had improved greatly. As the 2005 preseason wore on, Tony began to pull away from Henson. He finished the preseason with solid statistics, having completed 23 of 37 passes for 273 yards and a touchdown. More important, he had played his way into the backup role and even earned some consideration as a possible successor to Bledsoe.

Nonetheless, during his third regular season in the NFL, Tony once again failed to throw a single pass. Again he saw playing time only as the holder for a Cowboys team that finished 9-7 and once again fell short of the playoffs. He realized the clock was ticking, as he told Marc Narducci of the *Philadelphia Inquirer*:

❝I think at some point you think, 'Is it ever going to happen? It just might not be meant to be.' . . . I have always been a guy who looks toward the future and looks to getting better and working hard to get into a position to succeed when the time comes.❞

True to form, Tony had been working hard to improve, trying to set himself up to succeed when an opportunity finally presented itself. Clearly, though, everyone—including Tony himself—was beginning to question what the future held, and whether an opportunity would ever come. As a rookie, the kid from Eastern Illinois set out to improve his throwing mechanics and to find his niche in the National Football League. He had invested a lot of time and effort into becoming the quarterback that both Lee and Parcells wanted him to be, but as the 2005 season came to an end, he found himself still looking for his big break. Thankfully, he wouldn't have to wait much longer.

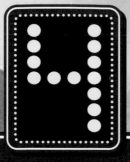

OVERNIGHT SENSATION

The clock was ticking, and Tony Romo knew it. He had been an NFL quarterback for three seasons now, but he had yet to throw a single regular-season pass. Thus far, the Cowboys had been patient waiting for him to develop, but they wouldn't wait forever. Essentially, it was now or never. Tony had to make his mark in 2006.

CROSS-CURRENTS

Tony Romo isn't the NFL's only successful quarterback to wait a long time before getting a chance to start. Read about two others on page 53. ▶▶

Cowboys coach Bill Parcells and owner Jerry Jones were both itching to return to the playoffs. The past couple of seasons had been unacceptable for a franchise with as storied a history as the Cowboys. The team made some big changes in the off-season, but none was bigger than the addition of wide receiver Terrell Owens.

An Uncertain Future

The signing of the flamboyant Owens—whose immense talent was undeniable but who had gained a reputation as a disruptive presence off the field during stints in San Francisco and Philadelphia—

As the 2006 season opened, Tony Romo again found himself in the backup role. But coach Bill Parcells was impatient to restore his team to the playoffs after two disappointing years. If Dallas stumbled, Parcells wouldn't hesitate to make changes—and that included shaking up the quarterback position.

dominated headlines in Dallas during the off-season. Owens vowed that his behavior would not be a distraction in the locker room. Still, some saw his acquisition as a sign of desperation on the part of Jones, who implied that nothing less than an immediate return to the playoffs would be acceptable. Coaches and players alike understood that failure to fulfill the owner's expectations would have consequences.

CROSS-CURRENTS

The Cowboys' long search for a quarterback of the future ended with the rise of Tony Romo. See page 54 to find out what happened to Tony's competition. ▶▶

This win-now mentality seemed to leave Tony Romo, once again, on the outside looking in. After all, as Jean-Jacques Taylor of the *Dallas Morning News* observed:

> **No coach wants to entrust his job to a free-agent quarterback who has never thrown a pass in a regular-season NFL game. I don't know that Tony will ever get a chance without the Cowboys' starter being injured. . . . I think he has talent . . . but I wouldn't hold my breath waiting for him to play.**

Tony Romo performed very well in the preseason, completing 69 percent of his passes. But Bledsoe played even better, hitting on 75 percent of his passes. Once again Parcells opted to open the regular season with his veteran at the helm of the offense. Still, Tony had convinced many Dallas fans, as well as football insiders, that his chance to start would indeed come—and perhaps sooner rather than later. Tony's fine play earned him a new two-year, $3.9 million contract. It also convinced the Cowboys' staff to release Drew Henson.

Seize the Day

During the fifth game of the 2006 season, Tony finally got a chance to play quarterback in a regular-season contest. He replaced Bledsoe late in the game—a blowout of the Houston Texans—and connected on both of his attempted passes, including a touchdown throw to Owens.

The victory over Houston gave Dallas a winning record of 3-2. Bledsoe had started all five games but had played erratically. So he was on a short leash entering the team's October 23, 2006, game

Tony scrambles away from defenders to pick up some yardage. In the fifth game of the 2006 season, the longtime backup finally got a chance to take a regular-season snap at quarterback. Two weeks later, after Drew Bledsoe had faltered, Tony was named the Cowboys' starting QB for the game against the Carolina Panthers.

against the New York Giants. The Giants held a 12-7 lead late in the first half, but the Cowboys were driving. Bledsoe threw a costly interception that prevented them from scoring, however.

Parcells had seen enough. When the team came out to start the third quarter, Tony Romo was at quarterback. Tony didn't engineer a storybook comeback—Dallas lost the game 36-22—and he threw three interceptions, including one that was returned for a touchdown. Still, he also connected for two touchdown passes, an 8-yard strike to Owens and a 53-yarder to Patrick Crayton. Tony's performance was promising enough that Parcells named him the Cowboys' new starting quarterback.

After Tony's sparkling performance against the Carolina Panthers, the Dallas Cowboys' faithful quickly embraced their team's new starting quarterback. Tony responded by leading the team to victories in six of his first eight starts. "Rarely in the annals of professional sports," noted one writer, "has a player shot from benchwarmer to superstar at such meteoric speed."

The Birth of Romomania

On the evening of Sunday, October 29, Tony Romo got the first regular-season start of his career. He and the Cowboys faced the Carolina Panthers in a nationally televised game. The pressure was on. Tony connected on his first two passes, both for short gains. But he was sacked on a third-**down** play and Dallas came up empty on its first possession. On the team's third drive, with the Cowboys trailing by a touchdown, Tony threw an interception that set up another easy score. At the end of the first quarter, Dallas trailed 14-0.

That's when it happened: Tony Romo took over the game. He connected on four of his first five passes to start the second quarter, including a touchdown pass to Jason Witten. Later in the quarter, he led the Cowboys on another drive that started at their own 12-yard line and culminated with a 38-yard field goal by kicker Mike Vanderjagt. After a scoreless third quarter, the Cowboys assumed command in the fourth, taking the lead on a second Vanderjagt field goal and then adding three additional touchdowns in a 35-14 victory. Football fans everywhere watched as Tony completed 24 of his 36 pass attempts for 270 yards and one touchdown. Most fans came away impressed.

Tony Romo became an overnight sensation. But as the season wore on, his play would only get better, and his star would shine brighter. After the victory over the Panthers, the Cowboys—despite an excellent two-touchdown performance by Tony—suffered a last-second loss to Washington. The following week, the young quarterback made sure his team rebounded from the heartbreaking loss with his first-ever 300-yard passing game, a performance that propelled Dallas to a 27-10 win over the Arizona Cardinals. For an encore, Tony led the Cowboys to an improbable 21-14 victory over the then-undefeated Indianapolis Colts. He followed that game up with his record-tying performance against Tampa Bay on Thanksgiving Day.

In all, Tony led Dallas to victories in six of the first eight games he started. He was voted to the **Pro Bowl**, the NFL's annual all-star game. If his on-field heroics weren't enough, Tony also started making headlines off the field. He became romantically linked to singer Carrie Underwood. Life was indeed good for Tony Romo, as Tim Madigan of the *Fort Worth Star-Telegram* observed:

> **"**Rarely in the annals of professional sports has a player shot from benchwarmer to superstar at such meteoric speed. One day, Tony Romo is an unknown athlete who played at a small university. . . . A few weeks later, he outduels the great Payton Manning . . . 'Romomania' is what the new affliction is called. He becomes North Texas' most eligible bachelor. But perhaps as remarkable as what Romo did on the field is how he did it—with a smile on his face, even during the tensest moments in the biggest games. It was like Texas Stadium and a national audience were no more daunting than the sandlots of Romo's Wisconsin childhood.**"**

Crashing Back to Reality

Just when it seemed that Romo could do no wrong, however, the wheels began to fall off. The Cowboys lost the final two games of the regular season. On Christmas Day, Tony had his worst game of the season. He completed just 14 of 29 passes and threw a pair of interceptions as the division rival Philadelphia Eagles administered a 23-7 spanking of Dallas. Then, on Week 17, Tony committed four **fumbles** and was picked off once, allowing the Detroit Lions to upset the playoff-bound Cowboys, 39-31.

Almost as suddenly as he had been dubbed the future of the Dallas Cowboys franchise, people began to question whether Tony really was ready for the task of leading the team at playoff time. Tony took it all in stride. As he told Clarence E. Hill Jr. of the *Fort Worth Star-Telegram*:

> **"**I understand it's my first year, and I'm not going to do everything right all the time. But I remember people questioning Peyton Manning, the most complete quarterback in the league. If they question a guy like that, anybody can be questioned. I am going to learn . . . and try to get better. What I tell people is it's not how you start, it's how you finish. . . . We are getting to that point in the season where it's time to finish.**"**

Nothing could quite prepare Tony for what happened next. Dallas traveled to Seattle to meet the Seahawks in the opening round

For a time, Tony dated singer Carrie Underwood. The two are seen here at the 42nd Academy of Country Music Awards, held at the MGM Grand in Las Vegas, Nevada, May 15, 2007. That night, the talented Underwood took away awards for top female vocalist, album of the year, and video of the year.

Season-ending fumble: Placekicker Martin Gramatica shuffles his feet as Tony drops the snap on a 19-yard field goal attempt late in the fourth quarter of the NFC wild card playoff game, January 6, 2007. Tony's mistake enabled the Seattle Seahawks to squeak by Dallas, 21-20. Afterward, a dejected Tony told reporters, "I don't know if I ever felt this low."

of the playoffs. It was a hard-fought contest. Tony performed solidly if not spectacularly, passing for 189 yards and one touchdown. Most important, however, he had Dallas in a position to win the game. With less than five minutes to play, Seattle scored a touchdown to take a one-point lead. But Tony drove the Dallas offense downfield, all the way to Seattle's two-yard line. On fourth down, with 1:19 left on the clock, Parcells sent Martin Gramatica, his new field goal kicker, onto the field to seal the win for the Cowboys.

The 19-yard kick—shorter than an extra point—should have been automatic. As always, Tony was the holder. The **snap** was good, but as Tony went to place the ball down, it slipped through his fingers. He desperately picked up the ball and scrambled toward the end zone. But he was tackled at the two-yard line, just inches short of a first down. The Seahawks won the game, 21-20. Tony was devastated by what the press would call one of the most memorable blunders in playoff history. "I don't know if I have ever felt this low," he told reporters after the game. But Tony wasn't making any excuses:

> **"I know how hard everyone in that locker room worked to get themselves in position to win that game today and for it to end like that, and for me to be the cause is very tough to swallow right now. I take responsibility for messing up at the end there. That's my fault. I cost the Dallas Cowboys a playoff win, and it's going to sit with me a long time."**

In many ways, 2006 was a dream season for Tony Romo. His years of hard work and patience had finally paid off. Earning his chance to start, he had led Dallas on an improbable run into the playoffs. Yet with a single snap, and one fumbled football, the dream turned into a nightmare. Tony was still the same talented young quarterback who had given the Cowboys a much-needed boost. But the season-ending mistake would haunt him, leaving experts to wonder if he would ever be the same.

AMERICA'S TEAM, AMERICA'S QUARTERBACK

The 2006 season had been a roller-coaster ride for Tony Romo. On the one hand, he had enjoyed the highs of winning the starters' job in Dallas and becoming a star on and off the field. On the other hand, he had suffered through the lows of playing poorly late in the season and then killing his team's playoff run.

CROSS-CURRENTS

Will Tony Romo eventually rank among the Cowboys' all-time great quarterbacks? Turn to page 55 to read about Hall of Famers Roger Staubach and Troy Aikman. ▶▶

With guard Marco Rivera providing protection, Tony drops back in the pocket and looks downfield for an open receiver. Sportswriters and Dallas Cowboys fans alike wondered whether Tony would bounce back from his season-ending muff in the wild card game against Seattle. He did, throwing for 36 touchdowns against only 19 interceptions in 2007.

There was much debate among football fans and media pundits about Tony's future. What kind of lasting impact would the big blunder in Seattle have? Would he rebound, or would he be one of those athletes who encounter adversity and fold?

Certainly, the memory of the debacle in Seattle could have been devastating to Tony's confidence. However, his family simply wouldn't allow this. The other members of the Romo clan had the final word on the topic, according to Jason Cole of *Yahoo! Sports*:

❝[In January] when the family gathered after the Cowboys' loss in the playoffs, Tony got zinged pretty good by older sister Danielle. He was still feeling the pain of the botched snap. At a certain point, big sis had heard enough.

❝She said to Tony, 'Get off the cross, we need the wood,' Ramiro Romo said. In other words, suck up the pain and the embarrassment, it's time to move on.**❞**

Moving Forward

It was sage advice, and Tony listened. Rather than continuing to reflect on his season-ending mistake, Tony decided to spend some of his off-season chasing another goal. He was trying to get into the 2007 U.S. Open golf tournament by playing a qualifying round in Irving, Texas. Tony had long been an avid golfer. In fact, he had

A devoted golfer since childhood, Tony attempted to win a spot in the 2007 U.S. Open field. However, in a qualifying round in Irving, Texas, Tony proved that he is no Tiger Woods. He completed the round at one over par, finishing out of the top 10 and falling short of his goal of playing in the U.S. Open.

attempted to qualify for PGA Tour events before. Again, however, he fell short. Tony finished at one over par and failed to place in the top 10. It was probably for the best, though. His day job was going to require the bulk of his attention.

The Cowboys faced some big changes during the off-season. On January 22, 2007, head coach Bill Parcells resigned. Team owner Jerry Jones interviewed many candidates, including former Cowboys offensive coordinator Norv Turner and one-time Dallas quarterback Jason Garrett, before hiring former Denver Broncos and Buffalo Bills head coach Wade Phillips. Garrett joined the staff as offensive coordinator. All this meant that Tony and his teammates would have to work hard during the preseason to learn a new offense. Following a 2-2 preseason, the new-look Cowboys made their 2007 debut at home on September 9 against the NFC East division rival New York Giants.

On his team's first possession, Tony led the Cowboys down the field on a 14-play drive that culminated in a field goal. Then, in the second quarter, Dallas scored 14 points, half coming as the result of Tony's first touchdown pass of the season, a 12-yard toss to Jason Witten. The Cowboys trailed by a point at halftime, but as the game wore on, the offense began to look more and more impressive. Tony hit Terrell Owens on a scoring pass early in the third quarter, then ran for another touchdown late in the period. By the time the game was over, Tony had accounted for five touchdowns and had thrown for a career-high 345 yards. He had guided the Cowboys to a 45-35 win over New York. So much for Tony's confidence being destroyed. He was back and better than ever.

The Start of Something Special

Tony led the Cowboys to victories in their first five games of 2007. He threw a pair of touchdown passes in a Week 2 victory over Miami, then followed that up with a 329-yard performance in a 34-10 thrashing of Chicago. Tony also topped the 300-yard mark in each of his next two games, throwing for a combined 648 yards and tossing a total of five touchdown passes in victories over the St. Louis Rams and the Buffalo Bills.

Of course, he still wasn't perfect. His performance against Buffalo was marred by five interceptions. He also turned in a subpar performance on October 14, as the New England Patriots handed Dallas its first loss of the season. Overall, however, Tony was playing very well—well enough, in fact, to convince Jerry Jones that he was the Cowboys' franchise quarterback. Before the end of October, Jones had rewarded Tony with a new six-year, $67.5 million contract. As Tony told ESPN.com News Services:

> **"I feel like I'm going to be with the Cowboys the rest of my career, definitely. I love it. . . .**
> **"It's a great feeling you have when the organization and the people stand behind you, and you can be the quarterback for a long, long time. It's a neat feeling that, 'You're our guy, we like you.' . . . It makes you feel good as a person and a player."**

With business matters out of the way, Tony could focus completely on football, and he continued to excel. He led Dallas to five wins during the month of November, culminating in a playoff-clinching victory at home against Brett Favre and the Green Bay Packers on November 29. In that contest, Tony completed 19 of his 30 attempted passes for 309 yards and four touchdowns. Through the first 12 games of 2007, Tony had thrown 33 touchdowns, shattering the previous Dallas single-season record of 29—and he had 4 games left to add to this total.

His achievements on the gridiron were eclipsed only by his increasingly high profile off the field. The athlete who had once dated Carrie Underwood (they had since broken up) was slowly becoming a pop-culture sensation. Recent tabloid reports had linked him romantically with several other starlets, including actress Sophia Bush and singer Britney Spears. Whether or not all these rumors were true, by this time there was a new woman in Tony's life—singer and actress Jessica Simpson.

Distraction, Dissension, and Disappointment

December would not be as kind to Tony Romo as previous months had been. Dallas managed only a 2-2 record during its four games in the final month of 2007. Worse yet, Tony's personal and professional lives were on a collision course. On December 16, television cameras caught Simpson at the team's home game against the Philadelphia

Tony celebrates a touchdown pass with members of his offensive line and running back Julius Jones. Powered by Tony's outstanding play at quarterback, Dallas scored more points during the 2007 regular season than any other NFL team except the undefeated New England Patriots. The Cowboys cruised to a regular-season record of 13-3, easily winning the NFC East division.

Tony Romo and girlfriend Jessica Simpson outside a club. The quarterback's relationship with the pop star was the subject of much tabloid copy. It also fueled controversy among sportswriters, broadcasters, and hard-core Dallas Cowboys fans—who wondered whether Tony's focus was really on the football field as playoff time approached.

Eagles, a 10-6 loss. A few days later, Tony's teammate Terrell Owens told reporters, "Right now, Jessica Simpson is not a fan favorite—in this locker room or in Texas Stadium." Owens further opined that Simpson was "taking [Romo's] focus away." The receiver later said that his comments were meant as a joke, but even if they were in jest, the media took hold of the story and simply would not let go.

Dallas finished the regular season with a 13-3 record and won the NFC East division title. As a reward to his team, Coach Phillips gave his players three days off before their playoff showdown against the New York Giants. Tony used that free time for a brief getaway with Jessica Simpson in the Mexican resort of Cancún. Little did he know, that would touch off a firestorm of controversy. Sportswriters and broadcasters were scathing in their criticism of the 27-year-old QB, questioning his focus and his dedication to his team. Romo brushed off the criticism, telling *Newsday.com*'s Erik Boland:

CROSS-CURRENTS

A native of Texas, Jessica Simpson is as celebrated in the Lone Star State as is her boyfriend Tony Romo. See page 56 for a profile. ▶▶

> **"If I don't perform well, it has nothing to do with anything other than the fact that the Giants played a better football game. . . .**
>
> **"This is my life. It's part of what goes along with being in this position . . . I try to do two things with my life. One is to work really hard in football. The other is to try and be a good person. If I do those two things, I can sleep at night, always."**

In a fairy-tale world, Tony would have come out and immediately silenced his critics with inspired play, leading the Cowboys to a playoff victory. That did not happen. Dallas was down by a touchdown before Tony and the offense even got the ball. His first two passes were incomplete. Dallas did rally, as Tony found Owens for a touchdown early in the second quarter, and running back Marion Barber scored later in the period. The game was tied 14-14 entering the third quarter, and the Cowboys added a field goal to take the lead into the game's final period. But a fourth-quarter touchdown run by Brandon Jacobs ultimately gave New York the victory. Tony had a mediocre game,

Tony Romo and Terrell Owens celebrate on the sidelines. During the Dallas Cowboys–New York Giants divisional playoff game, played at Texas Stadium on January 13, 2008, Romo and Owens connected for a second-quarter touchdown. New York had the last laugh, however, handing Dallas a bitterly disappointing 21-17 defeat.

completing half of his 36 pass attempts for 201 yards, and recording one touchdown and one interception. In the end, however, Dallas was left nursing the wounds of a disappointing finish to a once-promising season. The division rival Giants, meanwhile, would go on to win the Super Bowl.

Mission: Incomplete

The Tony Romo story thus far had been a most eventful tale. The kid who hadn't received a single Division I-A college scholarship coming out of high school was now fresh off a season in which he established new single-season Dallas Cowboys records for most touchdown passes (36), most passing yardage (4,211), and highest completion percentage (64.4), while also being named to his second-straight Pro Bowl. Following the 2007 season, Tony's star was shining bright. If he hadn't yet been recognized as one of the elite quarterbacks in the NFL, then he most certainly was on the cusp.

To be sure, he still had his critics, and those detractors were quick to point to his 0-2 playoff record. They accused him of being a playboy first and a quarterback second. But anyone who had closely followed the story of Tony Romo knew better. They knew of the extraordinary effort he had put forth to realize his dream of becoming a starting quarterback—both in college and in the NFL. They knew that the postseason struggles and the media criticism were simply a

Tony has given his time to various charitable causes. Here he clowns around with singer Kelly Clarkson to publicize the work of the Salvation Army, an organization that provides assistance to poor, elderly, sick, and addicted Americans. Clarkson, a Grammy Award winner, has served as an honorary chair of the Salvation Army.

With his on-field heroics and his winning personality, Tony Romo has captured the hearts of Cowboys fans. His chances of going down as one of the team's all-time great quarterbacks, alongside legends like Staubach and Aikman, will depend largely on whether he can bring another Super Bowl victory to Dallas.

few more challenges for the young man from Burlington, Wisconsin, to overcome. And, if the past provided a clue to the future, the odds were pretty good that Tony Romo would meet these challenges head on—and that he would succeed.

Football and Thanksgiving

Football and Thanksgiving seem to go hand-in-hand. For decades, NFL action has been as much a part of the holiday as turkey and cranberry sauce.

Much of the credit for beginning the tradition belongs to G. A. Richards. In 1934 Richards purchased the Portsmouth Spartans, moved the team to Detroit, and renamed the club the Detroit Lions. To generate fan interest in the club's new hometown, he decided to host a game on Thanksgiving. The Lions played the Chicago Bears that day, losing 19-16. But Richards's marketing ploy proved wildly successful. In fact, so many fans wanted to see the game that some had to be turned away at the gate. The Lions decided to make the Thanksgiving Day game an annual event.

Decades later Tex Schramm, the longtime general manager of the Dallas Cowboys, wanted to start a similar tradition with his club. On November 24, 1966, Schramm got his wish. In its first game on Thanksgiving, Dallas beat the Cleveland Browns, 26-14. Since then Dallas has hosted a Thanksgiving game every year, with the exception of 1975 and 1977. Entering the 2008 season, the Cowboys were 26-14-1 all time on Thanksgiving Day, with their most recent victory coming against the New York Jets on November 22, 2007. (Go back to page 4.) ◀◀

A performance by the Dallas Cowboys cheerleaders and the unfurling of a huge American flag were part of the Thanksgiving 2006 pregame show at Texas Stadium. Hosting a game on Thanksgiving has been a Cowboys tradition since 1966, but the Detroit Lions pioneered Thanksgiving Day football more than 30 years earlier.

Brad Childress, head coach of the Minnesota Vikings, walks off the field after a game. Like Tony Romo, Childress played his college football at Eastern Illinois University. So, too, did fellow NFL coaches Sean Payton and Mike Shanahan, who guided the Denver Broncos to back-to-back Super Bowl victories in 1997 and 1998.

Eastern Illinois University

Founded in 1895, Eastern Illinois University is a public school located in Charleston, Illinois. Its total enrollment is about 12,350. Of this number, approximately 10,600 are undergraduate students pursuing degrees in major subjects ranging from accounting, business administration, and finance to mathematics, chemistry, English, and African-American Studies. EIU also offers master's degrees through its College of Arts and Humanities, College of Education and Professional Studies, College of Sciences, and Lumpkin College of Business and Applied Sciences.

EIU has 21 sports teams. They compete either at the Division I level or at the FCS level. (FCS, or Football Championship Series, is the new name for Division I-AA football.) Most EIU teams, including the baseball, men's and women's basketball, and football teams, compete in the Ohio Valley Conference. The men's soccer team plays in the Missouri Valley Conference. The men's and women's swimming and diving teams compete in the Mid-Continent Conference, and the women's rugby team competes as an independent.

Although not known as a collegiate-sports powerhouse, Eastern Illinois has won six team national championships since 1899. In 1968 and 1969 the Panthers took back-to-back national titles in men's cross-country; another cross-country championship was added in 1977. Other national titles for the Panthers came in 1969 (men's soccer), 1974 (men's outdoor track), and 1978 (football).

Distinguished Graduates

Eastern Illinois has produced many famous and successful graduates. In addition to Tony Romo, three Panthers alumni have made their mark in the NFL: head coaches Mike Shanahan (who guided the Denver Broncos to two Super Bowls), Sean Payton, and Brad Childress. Basketball star Kevin Duckworth played 13 seasons in the NBA. As major league baseball players, pitcher Marty Pattin and third baseman Kevin Seitzer were both selected for All-Star teams. Track star John Craft set the U.S. record in the triple jump. Dan Steele won a bronze medal in the four-man bobsled at the 2002 Winter Olympics. Matt Hughes is an Ultimate Fighting Championships (UFC) world champion.

In the world of entertainment, Eastern Illinois has produced several notable actors. John Malkovich's numerous films include *In the Line of Fire* (1992), *Con Air* (1997), and *Beowulf* (2007). Joan Allen has starred in such movies as *Nixon* (1995), *The Bourne Supremacy* (2004), and *The Bourne Ultimatum* (2007). Jerry Van Dyke was a television sitcom actor.

Other famous Eastern Illinois graduates include former Illinois governor Jim Edgar, conservationist and animal rights activist Joan Embrey, and World War II veteran and Silver Star recipient Joe Snyder. (Go back to page 13.) ◀◀

The QB Class of 2003

Each year, scouts from all 32 NFL teams scour the ranks of college football programs, looking for promising prospects. These scouts, and the coaches and general managers of the NFL, may be excellent judges of football talent. But they frequently make mistakes. Often they draft players who never make it big in the pros, and occasionally they completely overlook a college player who goes on to have a stellar professional career. In 2003, for example, no team drafted Tony Romo, who has enjoyed a more successful early career than other quarterbacks drafted that year.

The first overall pick in the 2003 draft, Carson Palmer, has performed well quarterbacking the Cincinnati Bengals. Palmer, winner of the Heisman Trophy as college football's best player during his senior year at the University of Southern California, has already set several Bengals team records, including most **completions**, passing yards, and touchdown passes in a season.

By contrast, the second quarterback selected in the 2003 draft, Byron Leftwich, proved to be a major disappointment. A first-round pick of the Jacksonville Jaguars (and the seventh pick overall), Leftwich had four lackluster and injury-prone seasons with the Jaguars before being released in 2007. After a year with the Atlanta Falcons, he was again cut.

The Baltimore Ravens used the 19th pick in the first round on Kyle Boller. Boller, the third quarterback selected in the 2003 draft, has been mediocre through five seasons with the Ravens. He started all 16 games in his second year in the NFL, but later lost his starting job to Steve McNair. As of 2008, Boller had thrown about the same number of touchdown passes (45) as **interceptions** (44).

Rex Grossman, the next quarterback selected, has enjoyed some success (for instance, he completed 20 of 28 passes for the Chicago Bears in a losing effort in Super Bowl XLI). But he has also been wildly inconsistent. Entering the 2008 season, Grossman had thrown more interceptions (33) than touchdowns (31) as a pro.

Other quarterbacks drafted in 2003 had virtually no impact in the NFL. They include Dave Ragone, a third-round draft pick of the Houston Texans; Brian St. Pierre, drafted by the Pittsburgh Steelers in the fifth round; Kliff Kingsbury, a sixth-round selection by the New England Patriots; and Gibran Hamdan, picked by the Washington Redskins in the seventh round. (Go back to page 15.) ◀◀

Cincinnati Bengals quarterback Carson Palmer prepares to throw a pass. Palmer, a Heisman Trophy winner at the University of Southern California, was the first player selected in the 2003 NFL draft. In his first four years as a starter, Palmer threw for more than 100 touchdowns, including 32 in 2005, a year in which he was intercepted only 12 times.

The Big Tuna

Bill Parcells, nicknamed "the Big Tuna" during his tenure as linebackers coach of the New England Patriots, was undoubtedly one of the primary influences on Tony Romo's early NFL career. By the time he became the Cowboys' head coach in 2003—Tony's first year in the NFL—Parcells had earned a reputation as a strict taskmaster who got the best out of his players.

Born on August 22, 1941, in Englewood, New Jersey, Parcells played collegiate football at Wichita State. He coached at several colleges before taking his first NFL job, as defensive coordinator of the New York Giants, in 1979. In 1983 he became head coach of the Giants. Three years later he took the team to its first-ever Super Bowl victory. Parcells led his 1990 Giants to another Super Bowl win, but after that season he retired from coaching because of health problems.

The retirement would be short lived. Parcells resumed his coaching career in 1993 with the New England Patriots. After four seasons in New England, he became head coach of the New York Jets, a team he led for three years before going to Dallas. By the time of his second retirement, in 2006, Parcells had compiled a career regular-season coaching record of 172-130-1 and a post-season record of 11-8. (Go back to page 17.) ◀◀

Bill Parcells took over as head coach of the Dallas Cowboys in 2003, the same year Tony Romo entered the NFL. By then Parcells already had 15 years of experience as a head coach. The highlights of his coaching career were two Super Bowl wins, both with the New York Giants.

Delay of Game

Tony Romo waited three full seasons before getting an opportunity to throw his first regular-season NFL pass, but he is not alone. Plenty of great NFL quarterbacks had to bide their time for their chance at glory. Consider NFL Hall of Famer Steve Young. Young began his NFL career in 1985 with the Tampa Bay Buccaneers but played very little. Traded to the San Francisco 49ers in 1987, he found himself backing up the legendary Joe Montana. Young finally got his first chance to start an NFL game four years later, after Montana was injured. He went on to earn seven consecutive Pro Bowl selections, win two league MVP awards, and lead his team to victory in Super Bowl XXIX. Young retired with the highest quarterback rating in NFL history.

Brett Favre, drafted in 1991 by the Atlanta Falcons, also began his career on the bench. Falcons coach Jerry Glanville once reportedly said it would take something like a plane crash for him to allow Favre into a game. Traded to the Green Bay Packers in 1992, Favre went on to establish himself as one of the greatest quarterbacks in NFL history. By the time he retired in 2008, Favre had led the Packers to a Super Bowl win and set NFL career records in passing yards and touchdowns. (Go back to page 26.) ◀◀

San Francisco 49ers quarterback Steve Young drops back to pass in a game against the Washington Redskins. Young backed up the legendary Joe Montana for four years, finally becoming the 49ers' number-one QB at the age of 30. Still, he managed to put together a Hall of Fame career before retiring at 38.

Whatever Happened To . . .

In 2006 Tony Romo played his way into the starting lineup, earned a selection to the Pro Bowl, and appeared to have ensured his status as the Dallas Cowboys' quarterback of the future. So whatever happened to the other young quarterbacks with whom he competed in Dallas?

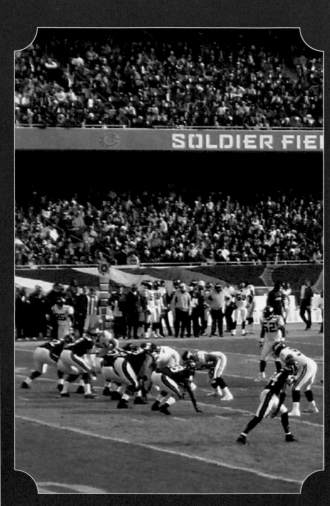

Chad Hutchinson quarterbacks the Chicago Bears in this December 5, 2004, game against the Minnesota Vikings at Chicago's Soldier Field. Hutchinson, once ahead of Tony Romo on the Cowboys' depth chart, started five games for the Bears during the 2004 season. But his play was erratic, and Chicago released him before the start of the 2005 season.

Following his dramatic release from the Cowboys, Quincy Carter signed with the New York Jets. He started three games for his new team after the Jets' number-one quarterback, Chad Pennington, suffered an injury. During the 2004 playoffs, Carter failed a drug test. He officially retired from the National Football League in September 2005. On October 12, 2007, he was arrested for marijuana possession, for which he faced felony charges as a repeat offender.

Chad Hutchinson signed with the Chicago Bears following his release by Dallas. Like Carter, Hutchinson was given an opportunity to start because of an injury to the number-one quarterback, Rex Grossman. However, thanks to poor play during the preseason, Hutchinson was quickly demoted in favor of Kyle Orton. He started five games for Chicago before being released. As of 2008 Hutchinson was, like Carter, out of football.

So, too, was Drew Henson, who was cut by the Minnesota Vikings in August 2007. In October of that year he got a tryout with the Jacksonville Jaguars but was passed over in favor of Todd Bouman. (Go back to page 28.) ◀◀

Following in Their Footsteps

Living up to the standards set by Dallas Cowboys quarterbacks of the past will be no easy task for Tony Romo. Over the years, the Dallas offense has been led by a couple of all-time greats of the game.

Any discussion of legendary Cowboys quarterbacks must begin with Hall of Famer Roger Staubach. In 11 seasons with Dallas (1969–1979), Staubach garnered six Pro Bowl selections, threw for 22,000 career yards, won two Super Bowls, and was named MVP of Super Bowl VI. Staubach's frequent late-game heroics earned him the nickname "Captain Comeback." He retired with what was then the highest QB rating in NFL history.

Like Staubach, Troy Aikman is a Hall of Famer and a former Super Bowl MVP, earning the honor in Super Bowl XXVII—one of the three Super Bowl victories Aikman helped bring to Dallas. During his long career with the Cowboys (1989–2000), he tied or broke 47 team records. The six-time Pro Bowler threw for nearly 33,000 yards, more than any other player in Dallas history, and was honored with the 1997 Walter Payton Man of the Year Award. (Go back to page 36.) ◀◀

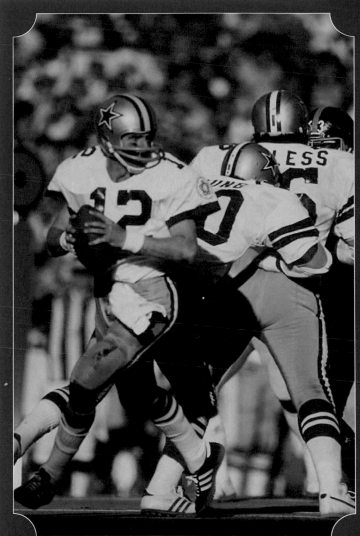

The elusive Roger Staubach rolls out during an NFC Championship game pitting Dallas against the Los Angeles Rams, January 4, 1976. The Cowboys won the game, 37-7. Staubach, who led Dallas to two Super Bowl victories during his illustrious 11-year pro career, was arguably the franchise's best quarterback ever.

Jessica Simpson

Tony Romo's girlfriend, Jessica Simpson, is no stranger to the spotlight. The popular singer and actress, born in 1980 and raised in Dallas, burst onto the music scene in 1999 with the release of her debut CD, *Sweet Kisses*. The album went double platinum, with the single "I Wanna Love You Forever" reaching the No. 3 spot on the Billboard Hot 100 chart. She followed up with 2001's *Irresistible* and the quadruple-platinum 2003 release *In This Skin*. Along the way, she married fellow singer Nick Lachey, and the duo began filming an MTV reality show about their marriage, entitled *Newlyweds*.

The couple gained immense fame, also starring together in a 2004 variety show. About a year later, however, their marriage had begun to disintegrate, and the two would divorce in 2006.

By this time, Simpson had made her motion picture debut, in 2005's *The Dukes of Hazzard*. Other movies included *Employee of the Month* (2006) and *Blonde Ambition* (2007). As of 2008, she had filmed eight movies and released six albums.

Simpson also works closely with Operation Smile, a nonprofit organization that provides corrective surgery for children with facial deformities. She and Tony Romo began dating in November 2007. (Go back to page 43.) ◀◀

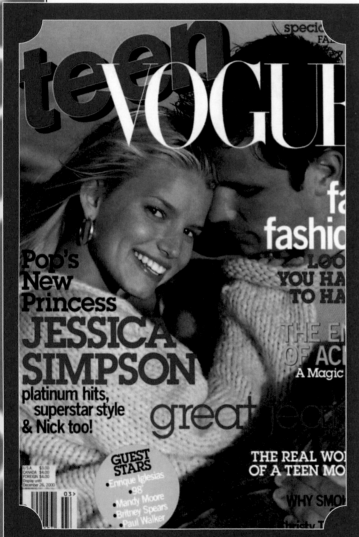

When Teen Vogue *magazine debuted in 2000, the cover featured pop sensation Jessica Simpson. The Texas-born singer, who at the time was only 20 years old, already had a double-platinum CD to her credit: 1999's* Sweet Kisses. *Since then Simpson has released several other big-selling CDs and appeared in a handful of movies.*

1982 Antonio Ramiro Romo is born on April 21 in San Diego, California.

1984 The Romo family moves from San Diego to Burlington, Wisconsin, where Tony spends most of his childhood.

1998 Enrolls at Eastern Illinois University; redshirts during his true freshman season.

1999 Sees his first NCAA action, playing in three games.

2000 Is named the Eastern Illinois starting quarterback and wins the first of three straight Ohio Valley Conference Player of the Year honors.

2001 Leads all Division I-AA quarterbacks in passing efficiency.

2002 In his senior year, earns consensus All-American honors and wins the Walter Payton Award as the best offensive player in Division I-AA football.

2003 Signs with the Dallas Cowboys as a rookie free agent on May 1.

2005 In his third season, beats out Drew Henson to become the Cowboys' backup quarterback; serves as holder on extra points and field goals.

2006 Replaces Drew Bledsoe as the starting quarterback after six games, playing well enough to be voted into the NFL Pro Bowl.

2007 Becomes the first Cowboys quarterback to throw for more than 4,000 yards in a season, leading Dallas into the playoffs and earning his second consecutive Pro Bowl berth. Also begins dating singer/actress Jessica Simpson.

Career Statistics

Year	Team	G	Att	Comp	Pct	Yds	TD	Int	QB Rating
2006	**Dallas**	16	337	220	65.3	2,903	19	13	95.1
2007	**Dallas**	16	520	335	64.4	4,211	36	19	97.0
TOTAL			**857**	**555**	**64.8**	**7,114**	**55**	**32**	**96.5**

Team Records

2006 Most touchdown passes, single game: 5 (November 23) (tied with Troy Aikman)

2007 Most completions, single season: 335

Most passing yards, single season: 4,211

Most passing touchdowns, single season: 36

Most games with 300-plus passing yards, single season: 7

Awards and Championships

2000 AP All-America Honorable Mention; Ohio Valley Conference Player of the Year; All-Ohio Valley Conference

2001 AP All-America Third Team; Ohio Valley Conference Player of the Year; All-Ohio Valley Conference

2002 Walter Payton Award; Consensus All-American; Ohio Valley Conference Player of the Year; All-Ohio Valley Conference

2006 NFL Pro Bowl

2007 NFL Pro Bowl

Books

Engel, Mac. *Tony Romo: America's Next Quarterback*. Chicago: Triumph Books, 2007.

Garrison, Walt. *Then Landry Said to Staubach: The Best Dallas Cowboys Stories Ever Told*. Chicago: Triumph Books, 2007.

Grabowski, John F. *Great Sports Teams: The Dallas Cowboys*. San Diego: Lucent Books, 2002.

Guinn, Jeff. *Dallas Cowboys: Our Story—The Authorized Pictorial History*. Arlington, TX: Summit Publishing Group, 1996.

Hawkes, Brian. *The History of the Dallas Cowboys*. Mankato, MN: Creative Education, 2004.

Luska, Frank. *Cowboys Essential: Everything You Need to Know to Be a Real Fan!* Chicago: Triumph Books, 2006.

Stewart, Mark. *Dallas Cowboys: A Team Spirit Book*. Chicago: Norwood House Paper Editions, 2007.

Taylor, Jean-Jacques. *Game of My Life: Memorable Stories from Cowboys Football*. Champaign, IL: Sports Publishing LLC, 2006.

Web Sites

http://www.dallascowboys.com/

The official Web site of the Dallas Cowboys includes team news, statistics, schedules, multimedia information, and much more.

http://www.nfl.com/players/tonyromo/profile?id=ROM787981

Tony Romo's page at NFL.com, featuring career stats, game logs, and video highlights.

http://www.nfl.com/

The official homepage of the National Football League.

http://www.pro-football-reference.com/

Pro-Football-Reference.com, a comprehensive collection of football statistics and player information.

http://espn.go.com/

The Internet home of the ESPN television network contains in-depth coverage of a variety of sports, including NFL football, as well as detailed information about various athletes and teams.

The Web sites mentioned in this book were active at the time of publication. The publisher is not responsible for Web sites that have changed their addresses or discontinued operation since the date of publication. The publisher will review and update the Web site addresses each time the book is reprinted.

attempt—a forward pass thrown by a quarterback.

completion—a pass that is successfully caught by the intended receiver.

down—one of four possible plays in which the offensive team must gain a combined total of 10 yards (thus earning a fresh set of four downs), score, or turn possession of the ball over to the opposing team. Usually expressed as a combination of down and distance remaining (for example, first and 10, second and 5).

draft—in sports, the annual process by which teams select new players from the college or amateur ranks, with teams that performed poorly during the past season picking before those with better records.

end zone—the area outside of the official 100-yard area of play, which the team on offense must reach in order to score a touchdown.

extra point—a kick, worth one point if the ball goes through the goalposts at the back of the end zone, that is attempted after a team scores a touchdown.

field goal—a kick, worth three points if the ball goes through the goalposts at the back of the end zone, that is generally attempted on fourth down.

free agent—a player who is not under contract and does not have an official commitment to any team, and who is therefore free to negotiate with any franchise he wishes.

fumble—the act of losing control of a football after having gotten legal possession of it.

gridiron—a slang term used to describe a football field.

holder—on field goal and extra-point attempts, the player who receives the snap, then turns and places the football on the ground for the kicker.

interception—a pass that is caught by a member of the opposing team.

passer rating—a statistic measuring the quality of a quarterback's play, determined through a formula consisting of completion percentage, yards per attempt, touchdowns per attempt, and interceptions per attempt. Also known as quarterback rating.

Pro Bowl—the NFL's annual all-star game, traditionally held in Hawaii the week after the Super Bowl.

redshirt—an athlete who may attend classes and practice with a team, but who may not participate in actual games, thus allowing the official start of a four-year college athletic career to be delayed.

rookie—a professional athlete who is playing in his or her first year.

snap—the act of starting a play by delivering the ball either to a quarterback, a holder, or another designated player.

touchdown—the act of scoring points by delivering the football into the opposing team's end zone, either by passing the ball or running with it. A touchdown itself is worth six points.

page 9 "The sky is the limit. . ." "Romo's Record Beats Bucs on Thanksgiving," NFL.com, November 23, 2006. http://www.nfl.com/gamecenter/recap?game_id=29022&displayPage=tab_recap&season=2006&week=REG12

page 9 "[Romo's] execution is good . . ." Nick Eatman, "Romo Has Career Day; Cowboys Rout Bucs, 38-10," Dallas Cowboys.com, November 24, 2006. http://www.dallascowboys.com/news.cfm?id=1817C71D-AE37-F6D9-A3BAE78BFE4C3BBB

page 12 "He studied so much . . ." Tom Silverstein, "Tony Romo Suddenly a Man in Demand, and Other Notes," *Milwaukee Journal Sentinel*, November 2, 2006.

page 12 "I would never . . ." Jason Wilde, "Star Status Really Hasn't Changed Tony Romo," *JG-TC Online*, November 26, 2007. http://www.jg-tc.com/articles/2007/11/26/sports/doc474b9f64cf63f479873280.txt

page 15 "Walter Payton exemplified . . ." Sports Network, "Tony Romo Wins the 2002 Walter Payton Award." http://www.sportsnetwork.com/default.asp?c=sportsnetwork&page=cfoot2/misc/2002payton_romo.htm

page 18 "It's definitely a different atmosphere . . ." Cliff Cook, "Scouting Report: Tony Romo," DallasCowboys.com, August 11, 2003. http://www.dallascowboys.com/scouting_report.cfm?scoutName=romo

page 18 "He kind of lives . . ." Mac Engel, *Tony Romo: America's Next Quarterback* (Chicago: Triumph Books, 2007), 70.

page 21 "There was no way . . ." Ibid., 73.

page 25 "I think at some point . . ." Marc Narducci, "Patience on Romo Becomes Virtue for Parcells," *Philadelphia Inquirer*, December 24, 2006.

page 28 "No coach wants to . . ." Jean-Jacques Taylor, "Witten Worth the Investment," CowboysPlus.com, July 25, 2006. http://www.cowboysplus.com/topstory/stories/072606cpivr.25b2c89.html

page 32 "Rarely in the annals . . ." Tim Madigan, "Man Behind the Mania: Tony Romo," *Fort Worth Star-Telegram*, December 31, 2006.

page 32 "I understand it's my first . . ." Clarence E. Hill Jr., "The Continuing Education of Tony Romo," *Fort Worth Star-Telegram*, December 31, 2006.

page 35 "I don't know if . . ." "Fumbles Help Seahawks Send off Cowboys," NFL.com, January 6, 2007. http://www.nfl.com/gamecenter/recap?game_id=29183&displayPage=tab_recap&season=2006&week=POST18&override=true

page 38 "[In January] when the family . . ." Jason Cole, "All in the Family," *Yahoo! Sports*, February 9, 2007. http://sports.yahoo.com/nfl/news?slug=jc-romo020907&prov=yhoo&type=lgns

page 40 "I feel like . . ." ESPN.com News Services, "Sources: Cowboys, Romo Agree on 6-year, $67.5 Million Deal," ESPN.com, October 30, 2007. http://sports.espn.go.com/nfl/news/story?id=3085827

page 43 "If I don't perform well . . ." Erik Boland, "Cowboy's QB Romo Enjoying His Star Power," *Newsday.com*, January 12, 2008. http://www.newsday.com/sports/football/giants/ny-spromo0113,0,6404384.story

page

5: SPCS Photos

6: Joe Robbins/Getty Images

8: Aggie Skirball/WireImage

11: ASP Library

13: Rob Brown/NFL/SPCS

14: Chris Graythen/Getty Images

17: IOS Photos

19: NFL/WireImage

20: Fort Worth Star-Telegram/MCT

23: Jed Jacobsohn/Getty Images

24: Streeter Lecka/Getty Images

27: Ronald Martinez/Getty Images

29: Dallas Morning News/MCT

30: Eliot J. Schechter/Getty Images

33: Getty Images

34: Fort Worth Star-Telegram/MCT

37: James D. Smith/WireImage

38: CCM/IOS Photos

41: Ronald Martinez/Getty Images

42: CIS Photos

44: Al Bello/Getty Images

45: Salvation Army/NMI

46: Jim McIsaac/Getty Images

47: SPCS Photos

48: Doug Pensinger/Getty Images

51: Andy Lyons/Getty Images

52: Dallas Morning News/MCT

53: NFL/WireImage

54: Chicago Tribune/MCT

55: Vernon Blever/NFL/SPCS

56: Teen Vogue/NMI

Front cover: Dallas Morning News/MCT

Front cover inset: Ronald Martinez/Getty Images

Chuck Bednar is an author and freelance writer from Ohio. He has written five additional books, including *Great Sports Teams: The San Antonio Spurs* (Lucent Books), as well as more than 1,300 published nonfiction articles. He is currently working as a forum administrator for GoTeamsGo.com.